THE TECH BEHIND
OFF-ROAD VEHICLES

Matt Chandler

Raintree is an imprint of Capstone Global Library Limited, a company incorporated in England and Wales
having its registered office at 264 Banbury Road, Oxford, OX2 7DY – Registered company number: 6695582

www.raintree.co.uk
myorders@raintree.co.uk

Edited by Carrie Braulick Sheely
Designed by Jennifer Bergstrom
Original illustrations © Capstone Global Library Limited 2020
Media research by Eric Gohl
Production by Katy LaVigne
Originated by Capstone Global Library Ltd
Printed and bound in India

ISBN: 978 1 4747 8826 7 (hardback)
ISBN: 978 1 4747 8830 4 (paperback)

British Library Cataloguing in Publication Data
A full catalogue record for this book is available from the British Library.

Acknowledgements
Alamy: Balan Madhavan/ARABIA, 8, FLHC 20, 7; AP Photo: Ross D. Franklin, 29; Dreamstime: Ermess,
11, Faki03, 12, Pavelvasenkov, 23; Getty Images: Focus on Sport, 5; Newscom: Icon Sportswire DHX/Shelley
Lipton, 18, UPI Photo Service, 4, ZUMA Press/Gene Blevins, 22, ZUMA Press/Rene Fluger, 26; Shutterstock:
Maciej Kopaniecki, 14, Mitrofanov Alexander, cover, Mohamed Alwerdany, 21, Nomad_Soul, 20, nuwatphoto,
10, otomobil, 24, PhotoStock10, 16, PPstock, 9, Risteski Goce, 13, stockphoto mania, 19, WORRAYUTH P, 15;
Wikimedia: Iannismardell, 25, Raphael Kirchner, 17. Design Elements: Shutterstock

CONTENTS

Evel Knievel attempts to jump the Caesars Palace fountains on his Triumph motorcycle in 1967.

CHAPTER 1

WILD RIDING OFF-ROAD

Robert "Evel" Knievel revved the engine of his Triumph motorcycle as thousands of fans cheered. It was New Year's Eve in 1967, and the daredevil was attempting his longest jump yet. Knievel was going to jump the world-famous fountains at Caesars Palace in Las Vegas, USA. The distance was 43 metres.

At first, it looked like he would make the jump. But he fell short and was violently thrown from the bike. He broke 40 bones in his body!

Robbie Knievel jumps over the Caesars Palace fountains on a dirt bike in 1989.

Knievel used motorcycles designed to ride on roads for his stunts. They didn't have the technology needed to handle huge jumps. But he didn't let this lack of technology stop him. He jumped everything from a line of buses to a tank full of live sharks!

Off-road vehicles are designed to be used off paved public streets. They can cope with huge jumps and rough landings. Could Knievel have cleared the fountains at Caesars Palace with better off-road technology? It's very likely. In 1989, his son, Robbie, jumped them successfully on a lightweight Honda dirt bike.

Many off-road options

Dirt bikes and all-terrain vehicles (ATVs) are two of the most popular types of off-road vehicles, but there are many others. Dune buggies are small vehicles with wide tyres designed to speed across sand and deserts. Since the early 1940s, armies have used jeeps to travel over rough land. Over time, the four-wheel-drive vehicles became available for anyone to buy.

History of off-road vehicles

The history of off-road vehicles varies depending on the type of vehicle. But their history goes side by side with the invention of the car in the late 1800s. Cars travelled over bumpy dirt roads. People began looking for ways to help them travel better on these rough roads. In 1893, Bramah Joseph Diplock made a four-wheel-drive system for a steam engine. In 1903, the Spyker company released an oil-powered car with four-wheel drive.

Vehicles fitted with Adolphe Kegresse's track could travel across snow. People sometimes added skis to the front of the vehicles.

Adolphe Kegresse is known as one of the world's first off-road vehicle inventors. In 1905, Kegresse began working for the Russian government. He made a system of tracks that could fit over a car's rear wheels. The Russian army used the system on many of its vehicles. It helped the vehicles travel over rough ground.

all-terrain vehicle (ATV) vehicle with large wheels that travels easily over rough ground

four-wheel drive system that transfers engine power to all four wheels of a vehicle for better grip

paddles

Paddle tyres are often fitted on the back of dune buggies, while smoother tyres are used at the front.

CHAPTER 2

THE INS AND OUTS OF OFF-ROAD TECH

Dirt bikes, quad bikes and dune buggies may seem like very different vehicles. But most off-road vehicles share some common features. Tough tyres, frames and suspension systems are important parts.

dirt bike tread

Tyres

Off-road tyres are thick and designed with tread. The tyre thickness protects against tearing. Dirt bike tyres have knobbly patterns. These allow the tyres to dig into the ground. They provide a good grip.

Trail tyres are common on quad bikes. These tyres have treads that can cope with many types of land, or terrain. In mud, a rider might switch to mud tyres. These tyres have large ridges called lugs to help pull the quad bike.

Dune buggies often use sand tyres. A sand tyre has wide ridges that run across its entire width. The ridges are called paddles. They pull vehicles through soft sand.

suspension system system of springs and shock absorbers that absorbs a vehicle's up-and-down movements

tread series of bumps and deep grooves on a tyre

Many dirt bike and ATV riders underinflate their tyres to have more tyre surface in contact with the ground. This process is called "airing down". It helps the tyres get better grip, or traction. One risk of this practice is rim damage. A new tyre technology for dirt bikes helps lower this risk. Tubliss is a two-part air chamber tyre system. Inside the tyre, an inner bladder filled to a high air pressure protects the rim. It allows the main tyre to be underinflated without risk of damaging the rim.

Tube frames help reduce an ATV's weight.

FACT

In 2013, Polaris introduced an ATV with airless tyres. The tyres are designed with a hard rubber shell wrapped around a honeycomb-shaped centre. They never go flat.

The Husqvarna 450 is a popular dirt bike for racing. It has a steel frame.

The frame game

A vehicle's body parts, suspension and other parts all connect to the frame, or chassis. Off-road riding is hard on the vehicle, so riders need a strong frame. But riders also want a lightweight vehicle so they can reach high speeds quickly. A light vehicle is easier to manoeuvre than a heavy one. Steel and aluminium frames are popular for many off-road vehicles. Aluminium is much lighter than steel. But steel is more durable and easier to repair.

manoeuvre to move something into position

Steel and aluminium respond differently, too. When a dirt bike rider hits the ground after a jump, a steel frame bends and springs back. This action absorbs some of the energy from the impact with the ground. An aluminium frame transfers the energy to the fork and the suspension of the bike, making for a less smooth ride.

Some off-road vehicle manufacturers combine the two metals. The Yamaha Raptor 700R ATV has a hybrid frame. The strength of steel is combined with lightweight aluminium.

Along with its hybrid frame, the Yamaha Raptor 700R has lightweight aluminium wheels to reduce weight.

Super suspensions

Speeding across rugged terrain at high speeds means lots of hard landings. That's why off-road manufacturers invest so much in suspension systems. The suspension has two main parts,

an ATV shock absorber

the spring and the damper. The damper is inside the spring. It slows the compression of the spring to control the bounce of the vehicle. Many ATV and dirt bike shock absorbers have a container called a reservoir filled with oil. Another container in the shock absorber holds gas. The movement of the oil controls the bounce of the shock spring. The gas stops bubbles forming in the oil, which can reduce performance. This type of shock absorber is called a monotube.

compression pressing or squeezing together

fork long part at the front of a motorcycle that connects to the front wheel

When ATV riders go through a lot of mud, the engine fins can become clogged.

CHAPTER 3

AWESOME ENGINE TECH

The engine is the heart of a vehicle. Off-road vehicle designers build engines best suited to each vehicle type. Each design comes with a lot of cutting-edge technology.

Keeping engines cool

Most ATV, dirt bike and dune buggy engines are petrol- or diesel-powered. These engines create a great deal of heat. If engines aren't cooled, they can overheat and break down. Air or water can cool engines.

In an air-cooled engine, a series of fins extend from the engine. The fins are designed to tunnel air towards the engine to help cool it. The advantage of air-cooled engines is that they are less expensive to repair. The biggest disadvantage of this type of engine has to do with mud. If a rider kicks up a lot of mud or sand, the fins can become blocked. Blocked fins can reduce the engine's ability to cool down.

engine fins

Racing dirt bikes have liquid-cooled engines that perform well under extreme conditions.

Liquid-cooled engines are the most common type of engine in modern ATVs. A pump pushes a liquid coolant, such as a mix of antifreeze and water, through chambers around the engine. The coolant absorbs the heat and passes through a radiator. The radiator forces out the heat with a fan. Because the liquid is constantly moving, liquid-cooled engines keep a more consistent temperature than air-cooled engines do. An air-cooled engine can overheat at slow speeds because less air moves over the engine. A liquid-cooled engine will cool the engine consistently at all speeds.

Electric engines

As electric cars have gained popularity, so have electric off-road vehicles. An electric-powered vehicle has an electric motor. A rechargeable battery supplies electricity to power the motor. Electric engines have some advantages over oil-powered engines. They are very quiet compared to oil-powered engines. Electric ATVs can be helpful to gamekeepers who need to move quietly. Electric motors are also more environmentally friendly. They do not release pollutants into the air through their exhaust pipes like oil-powered motors do.

FACT
The Daymak Beast ATV has one of the longest ranges of electric ATVs. It can travel up to 362 km before needing to be recharged.

the Polaris Ranger electric ATV

environment air, water, trees and other natural surroundings

Small changes, big improvements

Some technology focuses on providing power. Honda updated its 2019 CRF450R dirt bike with extended exhaust head pipes. The head pipe is the section of the exhaust pipe that connects to the engine's cylinder head. By extending the pipes, Honda says its bike performs better at high speeds.

FACT
Manufacturers improve engines for their motocross racing bikes. The 2019 Kawasaki KX 450 has a launch control system. With the push of a button, it changes the timing of how the engine runs. The system helps riders speed up at the beginning of a race.

ATV WATERPROOFING

Many off-road ATV riders enjoy splashing through water. But when water gets into the engine, it can cause serious damage. Off-road riders sometimes fit their ATVs with different parts to avoid this problem. An exhaust-fording or a snorkel kit can stop water entering the engine through the exhaust system. Some riders seal oil, gas and other caps with a soft material called silicone to keep out water.

Other engine improvements increase durability. Dirt bike piston rings used to be made from cast iron that cracked easily. Today's piston rings are made using a process called gas nitriding. In this process, the ring is blasted with nitrogen, which hardens the metal. With the new rings, fewer engine repairs are needed.

cylinder hollow area inside an engine in which fuel burns to create power

On ATVs without electronic steering, it can be more difficult for riders to make turns.

CHAPTER 4

CONTROL AND PERFORMANCE IMPROVEMENTS

Performance and control are key parts of off-road riding. Good control can help riders avoid crashes. Performance upgrades can give a racer the extra power to win a race. As manufacturers make changes to their off-road vehicles, some riders make updates to their own vehicles.

Electronic steering

ATVs with standard steering take a lot of strength to turn. Today many ATVs come with electronic power steering (EPS). It does a lot of the work for riders. A control unit collects data from sensors in the ATV, including speed and what direction the wheels are being turned. This data is used to determine how much steering assistance is needed. The biggest downside of EPS is that it adds more weight to the ATV.

FACT
In 2006, Yamaha introduced EPS on its Grizzly 700 ATV. It was the first ATV with the system.

sensor instrument that detects changes and sends information to a controlling device

BJ Baldwin speeds over sand dunes in California, USA, in his Chevrolet Blazer. The vehicle is fitted with a fibreglass front end.

Reducing weight

Designers are constantly working to make off-road vehicles lighter. A light vehicle can reach high speeds quickly and improve a rider's control. As well as using lightweight frames, they also consider body material. Plastic is a common body material because it is lightweight. Today's dirt bikes even have plastic fuel tanks.

Some off-road riders replace plastic bonnets and other parts with fibreglass or carbon fibre parts. Fibreglass is made of thin threads of glass. Carbon fibre is made of thin threads of carbon. Both materials are strong and lightweight. Riders consider which material fits their needs best. Fibreglass flexes better than carbon fibre, but carbon fibre is stronger than fibreglass.

Off-road manufacturers and riders can reduce weight by replacing steel parts with lighter metals. For example, the 2018 Jeep Wrangler off-road vehicle uses aluminium instead of steel in its doors, bonnet and bumpers. Some riders replace steel bolts, springs and other parts with titanium ones.

A driver tests the off-road ability of a 2018 Jeep Wrangler.

Smart suspensions

ATV riders constantly make adjustments to the suspension to change how their machines handle. They want their setup to have neither too much stiffness nor too much cushion. In 2017, Polaris invented the Dynamix active suspension to help riders with these adjustments. It was the first intelligent suspension system for off-road riders. A computer in an ATV with this system monitors speed, steering wheel position, accelerator pedal position and other data.

The Dynamix suspension is available on ATV models such as the RZR XP Turbo.

THE ZAROOQ SANDRACER

What if a rider wants high performance both on-road and off-road? The Zarooq Sandracer 500 GT offers the best of both worlds. These rare cars cost £350,000 each, but buyers get some serious tech. The Sandracer has a V-8 engine that produces 525 horsepower. The engine pushes the vehicle to a top speed of 220 km per hour. The adjustable suspension can move between a low height for road riding and a higher one for off-road riding. The carbon fibre body is attached to a strong tubular frame.

The system automatically adjusts the suspension to react to the information. For example, the sensors know when the ATV has gone into the air, and the shock absorber adjusts to brace for impact. When a rider takes a corner at high speed, the outside shocks react to prevent body roll.

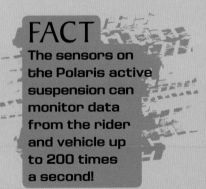

FACT

The sensors on the Polaris active suspension can monitor data from the rider and vehicle up to 200 times a second!

horsepower unit for measuring an engine's power

Hyundai showed off the Kite concept at the 2018 Geneva International Motor Show in Switzerland.

CHAPTER 5

THE FUTURE OF OFF-ROAD VEHICLES

Companies that design off-road vehicles are always making improvements and creating exciting new designs. While some of these designs are just for fun, others are designed for work.

Amphibious designs for the future

Imagine racing along a beach in your dune buggy. You head towards the water and press a button. In seconds, you're speeding through the waves. Today amphibious ATVs include the Gibbs Quadski and the Argo Frontier. Some companies are working on more amphibious vehicle designs.

Hyundai has designed a prototype called the Kite. It is a dune buggy that transforms into a jet ski. The Kite is an electric vehicle. Some amphibious vehicles have a system to power them over land and a separate one to power them over water. This setup can make the overall vehicle design bulky. The Kite has a single electrical system that powers the vehicle over both land and water. It allows the Kite to have a sleek body design.

STEALTHY BIKES

Companies have developed stealth dirt bikes as part of military research projects. These hybrid bikes can run on electric or oil power. Their electric motors make them almost silent. If they need fuel for a longer trip, they can run on olive oil!

amphibious vehicle that can travel over land and in water

prototype first version of an invention that tests an idea to see if it will work

stealth ability to move secretly

Self-driving tech

Off-road manufacturers are increasing self-driving features in off-road vehicles. One of the challenges rescuers face during a natural disaster is getting life-saving supplies to victims. Honda have designed a self-driving ATV to handle this job. The ATV has no rider. It uses sensors and cameras to "see" its surroundings. It's also fitted with a global positioning system (GPS). The on-board computer can be programmed to tell the ATV where to drive.

The ATV also has a driving mode called "Follow Me". It allows the ATV to be programmed to follow a leader. A lead vehicle or person carries a device that sends a signal to the ATV. The ATV follows the signal.

In 2018, firefighters tested the ATV in wildfires in Colorado, USA. The vehicle followed firefighters over rugged terrain. It carried supplies such as water tanks to remote areas.

Honda displayed its self-driving ATV designed to help with rescues at the 2019 Consumer Electronics Show in Las Vegas, USA.

More adventures to come

The technology for off-road vehicles has come a long way since the days when Evel Knievel took his road bike off-road. Modern tech gives riders a safer, more exciting off-road experience. The future of off-road riding is certain to be filled with adventure.

global positioning system electronic tool that receives signals from satellites to find the location of an object

GLOSSARY

all-terrain vehicle (ATV) vehicle with large wheels that travels easily over rough ground

amphibious vehicle that can travel over land and in water

compression pressing or squeezing together

cylinder hollow area inside an engine in which fuel burns to create power

environment air, water, trees and other natural surroundings

fork long part at the front of a motorcycle that connects to the front wheel

four-wheel drive system that transfers engine power to all four wheels of a vehicle for better grip

global positioning system electronic tool that receives signals from satellites to find the location of an object

horsepower unit for measuring an engine's power

manoeuvre move something into position

prototype first version of an invention that tests an idea to see if it will work

sensor instrument that detects changes and sends information to a controlling device

stealth ability to move secretly

suspension system system of springs and shock absorbers that absorbs a car's up-and-down movements

tread series of bumps and deep grooves on a tyre

FIND OUT MORE

BOOKS

STEAM Jobs for Petrolheads (STEAM Jobs), Sam Rhodes (Raintree, 2019)

The Impact of Technology in Sport (The Impact of Technology), Matthew Anniss (Raintree, 2016)

The World's Fastest Motorcycles (World Record Breakers), Ashley P. Watson Norris (Raintree, 2019)

WEBSITES

dkfindout.com/uk/science/materials/why-do-materials-work-in-different-ways/
Learn more about the different properties of materials, the impact the right material can have when designing new vehicles, and how scientists and engineers are developing techniques to make new materials.

sciencemuseum.org.uk/see-and-do/driverless-who-is-in-control
Discover driverless machines that already exist and how they are being further developed to make decisions on their own by interacting with this online exhibition, or visiting the Science Museum to take a look.

INDEX